Kingdom Living
Small Group Series

Worship...
Nearing the Heart of God

Kingdom Living
Small Group Series

Worship...
NEARING THE HEART OF GOD

ampelōn
PUBLISHING

Kingdom Living: Worship
Copyright ©2007 by Brian T. Anderson & Glynnis Whitwer

Unless otherwise noted, scripture quotations taken from the HOLY BIBLE, NEW INTERNATIONAL VERSION. NIV. Copyright © 1973, 1978, 1984 by International Bible Society. Used by permission of Zondervan Publishing House. All rights reserved.

Scripture quotations marked (NASB) taken from the New American Standard Bible®, Copyright © 1960, 1962, 1963, 1968, 1971, 1972, 1973, 1975, 1977, 1995 by The Lockman Foundation. Used by permission.

Scripture quotations marked (Message) taken from THE MESSAGE, Copyright © by Eugene Peterson, 1993, 1994, 1995. Used by permission of NavPress Publishing Group.

All rights reserved. No part of this publication may be reproduced in any form or by any means — electronic, mechanical, photocopy, recording, or any other — except for brief quotations in printed reviews, without the prior permission of the publisher.

ISBN: 978-0-9786394-1-9

Printed in the United States of America
First printing

Requests for information should be addressed to:
Ampelon Publishing
6920 Jimmy Carter Blvd., Suite 200
Norcross, GA 30071
To order other Ampelon Publishing products, visit us on the web at:
www.ampelonpublishing.com

Cover photo by Juan Gabriel Estey

Contents

How to use this study guide 7

Introduction to Worship 11

Lesson One:
Settling the Issue of Lordship 13

Lesson Two:
Experiencing God in Worship 19

Lesson Three:
Gaining a God-Perspective on Life 27

Lesson Four:
Developing Our Character Through Worship 35

Lesson Five:
Overcoming Our Hindrances to Worship 43

Lesson Six:
Advancing God's Kingdom Through Worship 51

Leader's Guide 59

The Kingdom Living Bible Study Series

The kingdom of God is not defined by mighty fortress walls, colorful pennants fluttering in the breeze, or mounted saints on powerful steeds. It's not a place where sentries patrol castle walls and moats deter intruders. The kingdom of God isn't a place we can visit, but it's as real as any empire known to man.

The kingdom of God is really a kingdom within a kingdom. It's a spiritual kingdom, ushered in by Jesus, where God reigns over everything. It is both a present reality and a future hope. And yet it exists in the midst of the kingdoms of this earth, where Satan rules.

The Israelites had been promised this kingdom of God, also referred to as the kingdom of heaven in the book of Matthew. They had been waiting thousands of years for the promised King who would restore them to power and save them from their suffering. So when John the Baptist proclaimed, "Repent, for the kingdom of heaven is near" (Matthew 3:2), they listened.

Jesus said those same words Himself in Matthew 4:17. In fact, the message of the kingdom of God was the reason Jesus said He came. When the people of Capernaum wanted Jesus to stay longer, He said, "I must preach the good news of the kingdom of God to the other towns also, because that is why I was sent" (Luke 4:43). Christianity did not start with the story of the resurrection of Jesus—that hadn't happened. People repented and turned to God through the teachings and the reality of the kingdom of heaven.

Jesus modeled the life of a subject of the kingdom of heaven. As He walked from city to city, He invested His life in others, taught, preached the good news of the kingdom, cared for the poor, healed the sick, and cast out demons. Jesus showed us that the kingdom of God is where God's Word is being taught and His work is being done.

As believers today, we are called to continue the works of Jesus and advance the kingdom of God. Jesus said, "Truly, truly, I say to you, he who believes in Me, the works that I do, he will do also; and greater works than these he will do; because I go to the Father" (John 14:12, NASB). However, as people of the Kingdom, we are also thrust into a war with God's enemies. How do we obey the commands of Jesus, yet battle an unseen enemy?

The key to walking in the power of the kingdom of God is learning to do what the Father is doing in each situation. Jesus Himself acknowledged His dependence on God: "Therefore Jesus answered and was saying to them, 'Truly, truly, I say to you, the Son can do nothing of Himself, unless it is something He sees the Father doing; for whatever the Father does, these things the Son also does in like manner'" (John 5:19, NASB).

In this Kingdom Living Bible Study Series, we will delve deeply into what living life as a follower of Jesus is all about. We'll study Scripture and apply the Word of God to our hearts and lives. We'll learn how to live like Christ, how to watch for what the Father is doing, experience transformation, and impact our community with the Good News of the Gospel.

Life in the kingdom of God is exciting! We invite you to pursue following Jesus with all your heart and get ready for an adventure. Kingdom living will transform your life.

SMALL GROUP TIPS

These studies are designed for personal or group studies. If you are participating in a group, we would like to share some tips for making it a great experience.

First, congratulations on taking this step to develop community with other believers! We weren't meant to be isolated Christians. After Pentecost, there were 3,000 believers in Jerusalem. Acts 2:42 says, "They devoted themselves to the apostles' teaching and to the fellowship, to the breaking of bread and to prayer." Imagine 3,000 believers, passionate about their love for God, meeting in homes for fellowship, teaching and prayer. Oh, yes, ... and food!

Small groups were one of the first ways the kingdom of God was advanced. Acts 2:46-47 tells us more about these first believers: "Every day they continued to meet together in the temple courts. They broke bread in their homes and ate together with glad and sincere hearts, praising God and enjoying the favor of all the people. And the Lord added to their number daily those who were being saved." Meeting in large groups, meeting in homes in small groups, praising God and sharing the Good News—what an amazing picture of community.

As you embark on this study, we encourage you to open your heart to what God might want to do during your small group time. Here are some ideas on how to prepare:

1. Before each group meeting, do your best to be prepared—pray about and get familiar with the content of that week's Bible study.

2. Pray for your group beforehand. Pray for your leaders, the hosts, and the other people in the group.

3. Watch for God to speak to you during the small group. This could be during worship, prayer, through another member of the group, or quietly in your heart.

4. Be open to meeting with people different from you. God may specifically put you in a group so you can learn from others with different experiences and insights.

5. Be transparent. You don't have to spill your guts, but be willing to share your personal struggles when appropriate. This is how trust develops in a group.

6. Be yourself. God has called you into His service just how you are. You don't have to try and be like anybody else. Guard your heart against comparisons.

7. Protect confidentiality. What is shared in the group, stays in the group.

8. Look for one idea to apply to your life today. Allow God's Word to change your life one small step at a time.

BIBLE STUDY BASICS

Studying the Bible can seem overwhelming. It doesn't have to be. Our goal with this series is to learn more about life in the kingdom of God bit by bit. God wants us to understand His Word and will open our ears and hearts when we approach Bible study with a willing heart. Here are some tips to get you started:

1. Pray before doing your lesson. Ask God to teach you from the Scriptures and to speak to you through the Holy Spirit.

2. Read the Scripture reference several times. If it's a familiar verse, read it out loud to gain a new perspective. Read it in different versions if you have them. (www.biblegateway.com and www.crosswalk.com offer many versions on line)

3. If you have a Bible with study notes, read them. Read any cross-references (often indicated by a small letter after a word).

4. Read with expectancy that God will teach you from His Word. Don't try to make the Scripture say what you want it to say.

5. Look for the main theme of each passage, look for the context (read before and after the verse), and identify how the central truth applies to you.

6. Answer the questions to the best of your ability. If you are unsure of an answer, that's OK. Share that with the group and ask for their help in understanding the passage or question.

7. Thank God for the gift of the Bible and for teaching you through it.

We pray that God will touch you in a deep and intimate way as you study His word and apply yourself to becoming a passionate follower of Jesus. May God bless you richly.

Worship...
NEARING THE HEART OF GOD

Have you ever felt like you're disconnected from God? Your heart is breaking and you feel far from Him? You wonder, "Where is God in all of this?" It's at those times, often when we feel least like praising God, that we need to focus on worship. The truth is that God never leaves us, but He is always waiting for us to draw near. When we worship God with our lips and our lives, we are nearer His heart than at any other time. In fact, Jesus told us God is not only waiting for us to worship Him, but He is seeking worshipers.

Jesus had been traveling and stopped for rest and a cool drink in Samaria. While the disciples spread out to find food, Jesus met a woman drawing water and asked for a drink. In typical Jesus fashion, the conversation quickly turned from H_2O to the abundant life Jesus could offer her. This passage is textured with meaning, and one theme is worship.

After having her private life uncomfortably revealed by a stranger, the woman abruptly changed the subject. Where, she wanted to know, was the right place to worship? Was it on a mountain where her ancestors worshipped, or was it in Jerusalem? Jesus' answer is rich and full. He tells her that a time is coming, and in fact was there, when "true worshipers will worship the Father in spirit and truth, for they are the kind of worshipers the Father seeks" (John 4:23).

This woman wanted to be right with God and assured that she was in the right physical place for worship—but Jesus wanted her in the right spiritual place. It didn't matter where she worshipped God from an outward perspective, but how she worshipped on the inside. Jesus moved worship from something we do, to someone we are: a worshiper.

It's easy to let familiar words breeze through our mouths, without our hearts being fully engaged in worship. We can even plan other things and sing praises at the same time. But when we worship in spirit and truth, our hearts are laid bare before the Lord. It's as if we open a door to the deepest place in our spirits and God steps in. It's in true worship that we near the heart of God and are forever changed.

Becoming a worshiper takes time and discipline. Our natural inclination is to focus on ourselves, rather than God. Yet God knows that true worship will change our lives, and He calls us to persevere.

Learning to become a worshiper deserves our best. As John Wimber wrote in All About Worship, "Becoming true worshippers is the chief assignment God has given us in this lifetime." We pray this Bible study inspires you to develop a heart for worship, overcome the obstacles to worship, and experience greater power as a follower of Jesus.

one
Worship
SETTLING THE ISSUE OF LORDSHIP

How worship helps us prioritize our lives

When he came near the place where the road goes down the Mount of Olives, the whole crowd of disciples began joyfully to praise God in loud voices for all the miracles they had seen: "Blessed is the king who comes in the name of the Lord! Peace in heaven and glory in the highest!" Some of the Pharisees in the crowd said to Jesus, "Teacher, rebuke your disciples!" "I tell you," he replied, "if they keep quiet, the stones will cry out."

Luke 19:37-40

By narrow definition, worship means to adore, idolize, or see as great worth. Although that happens on the inside, worship also involves action. Therein lies the danger for a believer. It is possible to go though the outward motions of worship without our hearts being fully engaged. We can sing, raise our hands, and even dance without really worshiping. But when we acknowledge God as Lord of our lives, worship is a natural overflow of the love in our hearts.

Many Christians come to know God first as their Savior. We oftentimes know we need help and willingly accept the gift of salvation Jesus offers. But, making Christ Lord is often a difficult step. Acknowledging the Lordship of Jesus in our lives means submitting ourselves and our wills to Jesus Christ—something that doesn't come naturally. Jesus isn't just a part of our lives; He should be leading, guiding, and influencing every part of the way we live. As difficult as it may be, settling the issue of who is Lord is crucial to living a full Christian life and the foundation of worship.

We worship what we are submitted to. Without being fully submitted to Jesus Christ, worship is simply singing nice songs and speaking empty words. If you haven't settled the issue of who is Lord of your life, let God speak to you through this lesson.

Many Christians come to know God first as their Savior. We oftentimes know we need help and willingly accept the gift of salvation Jesus offers. But, making Christ Lord is often a difficult step. Acknowledging the Lordship of Jesus in our lives means submitting ourselves and our wills to Jesus Christ—something that doesn't come naturally. Jesus isn't just a part of our lives; He should be leading, guiding, and influencing every part of the way we live. As difficult as it may be, settling the issue of who is Lord is crucial to living a full Christian life and the foundation of worship.

We worship what we are submitted to. Without being fully submitted to Jesus Christ, worship is simply singing nice songs and speaking empty words. If you haven't settled the issue of who is Lord of your life, let God speak to you through this lesson.

■ Let's Talk

1) What motivates you most when making everyday decisions? Why?

2) What are some decisions you've made lately that reflect this motivation?

■ Entering In

Read Exodus 20:1-4.
3) These are the first four verses in the delivery of the Ten Commandments. What is the first thing God does in verse two? Why would He introduce the Ten Commandments this way?

BytheWay ...

The Hebrew name for "Lord" is Yahweh. This means "He is" or "He will be." Interestingly, this is the third-person form of "I am," which was how God identified Himself to Moses in Exodus 3:14. When we call God "Lord," we are really saying "He is"!

---

4) In verse three, God calls His people to a decision of whom they will serve and worship. Why would God make this the first commandment?

5) We might dismiss this first commandment as irrelevant in today's culture. Most of us don't live among people who actively worship or make sacrifices to other gods. Yet we can willingly sacrifice time or money for things other than God. What are some examples in your life?

6) God requires that His people make Him first in every part of their lives. This isn't a selfish desire on God's part. How does making God first in every part of our lives benefit *us*?

BytheWay ...
An idol doesn't have to be a golden statue. And worshiping another god doesn't need to involve a pagan cult. An idol or god can be anything in your life that controls you, or anything you turn to on a regular basis for comfort besides God. For example, this can be a person, relationship, substance or even entertainment.

---

7) The second commandment God gives (v. 4) is about making idols. Based on the description in By The Way, what are some modern day "idols" or "gods"?

8) Why do these idols disappoint us?

Read Psalm 115: 2-8.
9) What does verse 8 say about those who make idols?

10) What application might this have for you when you choose to worship an "idol"?

Read Romans 12:1.
11) How is offering our body as a living sacrifice an act of worship?

■ Putting Feet to It

12) If we don't acknowledge Jesus as our Lord, can we really worship Him? Why or why not?

13) What changes do you need to make in your heart and in your life to begin allowing Jesus to lead, guide and influence the way you live every part of your life?

■ Taking It with You

Matthew 6:33: "But seek first his kingdom and his righteousness, and all these things will be given to you as well." (NASB)

■ Journal

two

EXPERIENCING GOD IN WORSHIP

How we touch the Father's Heart ... and He touches us

"Teacher, which is the greatest commandment in the Law?" Jesus replied: "'Love the Lord your God with all your heart and with all your soul and with all your mind.' This is the first and greatest commandment. And the second is like it: 'Love your neighbor as yourself.' All the Law and the Prophets hang on these two commandments."

Matthew 22:36-40

Imagine sitting across the table from your first love. You lean forward, eyes locked, intent on every word spoken and every emotion unspoken. Words flow freely as you experience a freedom to share your innermost thoughts and feelings. Your heart pounds as you speak of your love and devotion. Even after your time together has ended, the warmth of the intimacy you shared fills your heart. You sense your beloved's presence long after you've parted. Knowing you are loved in return fills you with great confidence.

Some may wonder, "Is that type of love possible?" The answer is, "Yes!" This sweet time of intimacy is God's desire for us each time we enter in to worship. In fact, loving God is our highest calling as a Christian. Jesus Himself told us it was the most important commandment: "Love the Lord your God with all your heart and with all your soul and with all your mind" (Matthew 22:37). When we express that love in worship, it's like God opens the gates of heaven and reveals Himself to His worshipers in greater measure.

Not only does God reveal Himself to us, but as we unlock the padlocks on our own hearts, God moves in to our deepest places. In worship, something supernatural happens. "Deep calls to deep" as the Psalmist wrote—we experience the deep places of God and discover a depth to our own souls.

Expressing our love and affection toward God, when we're not used to doing this, feels awkward. Yet when we push through our discomfort, we experience God in a richer way than we ever imagined. God does not play a hide-and-go-seek game with His followers. He longs to be discovered. When we enter fully into worship, we come to know God, and we experience being known.

■ Let's Talk

1) Think of someone with whom you find it easy to share your deepest thoughts and feelings. What makes that person so easy to talk with?

2) What matters more to you—to know someone intimately or be known intimately? Why?

■ Entering In

Read Hebrews 10:19-22.

Two: Experiencing God in Worship

BytheWay ...

In the Old Testament, only the High Priest could truly enter into the presence of God, and only on one day a year (the Day of Atonement). In fact, the presence of God dwelt in a section of the temple called the Holy of Holies. The temple was divided into 3 parts—the outer court, the inner court, and the Holy of Holies. The Ark of the Covenant was found there, and God's presence dwelt between the two cherubim on the Ark of the Covenant. The Holy of Holies was separated from the inner court by a six-inch thick "veil" or curtain. When Jesus died on the cross, this veil was ripped in two, thereby making it possible for all believers to experience God (Matthew 27:50-51).

---

3) As Christians today, we experience the joy of free access to God through reading His word or speaking to Him in prayer. How would your life as a believer be different if you couldn't know and experience God personally?

4) In the Old Testament, before Jesus came to earth, only the priests had access to God, and even that access involved an exact routine of preparation and sacrifices. This was because the holiness of God was so awesome that to approach Him carelessly could result in death. According to Hebrews 10:19-22, why do we now have free access to God? Describe what that means to you as a follower of Jesus.

5) These verses in Hebrews set us up for action. We are reminded that "since" we have confidence and "since" we have Jesus as our access to God, we can now do something. What is it believers can now do?

6) The verses also describe the conditions our hearts must be in to approach God. What are those conditions? Describe in your own words.

Read James 4:8.
7) This verse sets up an "if-then" situation. What must we do before God will draw near to us? Why would God wait for us to make the first move?

8) There's a second requirement found in the last part of verse eight. What are the two things we must do in order to experience God?

9) What are some practical ways you can prepare yourself to draw near to God?

Read Psalm 22:3.
10) When we worship together, God's presence comes and fills the room. Psalm 22:3 says that God is enthroned upon the praises of believers. "Enthroned upon" means to sit down, remain or abide. Why would God "sit down, remain or abide" on the corporate praises of believers?

11) Do you ever experience God in a greater way when corporately worshiping with other believers? What are some ways to cultivate that experience more often?

12) Jeremiah 29:13 says, "You will seek Me and find Me when you search for Me with all your heart." What does searching for God with "all our heart" mean?

ByTheWay ...

There are eight different words used for *worship* in the Bible. The one that's most common is the Greek word "proskuneo." This word is used 66 times in the New Testament, and it actually means to turn toward to kiss. Worship is often meant to be a very intimate experience of God.

Read 1 Chronicles 16:9a.
13) This verse gives us the key to experiencing God in worship. What is it?

14) When you sing to God, instead of about Him, what does that possibly say to God?

■ Putting Feet to It

ByTheWay ...

Here are three tips to help you experience God's presence in corporate worship: 1) Prepare yourself beforehand, even the day before, through prayer. 2) Get to church early. 3) Make a willful decision to focus on the Lord.

15) To make your worship more intimate, think about loving God in the same way you love those closest to you. In that case, what are words of love you might use when worshiping?

16) Think about a time when you felt the presence of God most strongly during worship. If you feel comfortable, share that experience with the group. What did you learn about God? About yourself?

■ Taking It with You

Jeremiah 29:13: "You will seek Me and find Me when you search for Me with all your heart." (NASB)

Journal

three
Worship
GAINING A GOD-PERSPECTIVE ON LIFE

How to see life and others like the Father

For you did not receive a spirit that makes you a slave again to fear, but you received the Spirit of sonship. And by him we cry, "Abba, Father."

Romans 8:15

Have you ever entered into worship with a heavy heart and lots of burdens, only to feel them begin to lift with each song? It's amazing how worship can do that, We come to church with our minds filled with our troubles, wondering how we're going to deal with them, and fearful of the future. Then something wonderful happens! In worship, when we turn our attention from our problems and onto the One who can solve them, we get a different perspective on life. We get a God-perspective.

As we sing worship songs that are rooted in God's Word and focus on His majesty, His great worth, and His all-powerful nature, we realize we aren't alone. When worship songs include Scripture, we plant God's Word in our minds and hearts. As we worship, we are reminded that Jesus will not only share our burdens but will actually remove them. Words about God's greatness convey His ability to do far more abundantly than we can ask or think. As we pour out our love for God, we feel His love in return. And in feeling that love, we experience the heart of a Father who delights in providing for our needs.

When our eyes are opened in worship, we have a clear vision of who we are, who God is, and why we need Him so desperately. In seeing who we are in light of God's greatness, we experience humility. How can so great a God love someone like me? Yet, we also experience our worth. Wow! A God so great loves someone like me! This is a healthy place to rest—confident that the arms of God are wrapped around us, and that He cares about every detail of our lives.

Gaining a God-perspective on life through worship allows us to walk through life with our heads held high—not as an orphan begging for a crust of bread, but as a son or daughter of the most high God. We can be sure that God cares about us and that God will act on our behalf. This brings great peace and comfort in the midst of a very uncertain world.

■ Let's Talk

1) Have you ever trusted someone completely? How did you display that trust? What did you trust that person with?

2) Describe something or someone that caused you to be in awe or wonder.

■ Entering In

Read Matthew 16:13-17.

ByTheWay ...

Jesus opens this passage with a question: "Who do people say the Son of Man is?" The term "Son of Man" occurs over 80 times in the Gospels and, with a few exceptions, is the only title Jesus uses for Himself. To our ears, it might seem like Jesus was attempting to be identified as a man. But Jesus' listeners would have known the Old Testament prophesy in Daniel chapter 7, which proclaimed that one day a "Son of Man was coming" who would be "given dominion, glory and a kingdom, that all the peoples, nations and men of every language might serve Him." In Mark chapter 14, verses 61-64 at the end of His ministry, Jesus identifies what He meant by the term Son of Man. "But He kept silent and did not answer. Again the high priest was questioning Him, and saying to Him, 'Are You the Christ, the Son of the Blessed One?' And Jesus said, 'I am; and you shall see the Son of Man sitting at the right hand of power, and coming with the clouds of heaven.'" Here in His last hours, Jesus declared that He was the prophesied one who has all dominion and power whom everyone will serve. The Sanhedrin understood that He was proclaiming that He was God and judged Him worthy of death for saying it.

3) Among the Jews in Caesarea Philippi, theories abounded about who Jesus really was. Why would Jesus ask Peter to list some of the theories?

4) After having Peter acknowledge the options, Jesus asks the most important question, "Who do you say I am?" By now, Jesus would have known the answer to this question. Why would Jesus ask Peter what He already knew?

5) What is Peter's answer?

6) When we acknowledge that Jesus is the Christ, the Son of the Living God, how does that change what we ask for in prayer?

7) Jesus' response to Peter shows that God Himself will help us understand who He is. How does worship help us understand the truth about God's character?

Three: Gaining a God-Perspective on Life   31

ByTheWay ...

Someone once said, "If your problems are too big, your God is too small." We can easily put limits on God by not understanding who He really is. In worship, God reveals His majesty and omnipotence (unlimited power) to us.

Read Isaiah 6:1-5.
8) Describe what Isaiah saw in his vision (vs. 1-2).

9) What are the seraphs saying? What happens at the sound of their voices?

10) Imagine if God allowed you to see a vision of His glory in such vivid detail. How might that change your perspective on life?

ByTheWay ...

The "seraphs" mentioned in this passage, are among the heavenly beings created by God. Other created beings include angels, archangels, cherubim and principalities.

---

11) When Isaiah sees the vision of God's glory, how does he respond?

12) Humility is a natural response when we fully experience God's glory. How is a healthy humility different from Satan's condemnation?

13) Scripture tells us that God gives grace to the humble (James 4:6). What is the opposite of humility? How does that hinder God's work in our lives?

Read Isaiah 6: 6-7.
14) In view of Isaiah's brokenness, what does a seraph do and say?

15) What hope do we have now when we are confronted with our own sin and brokenness? (Read Romans 7:24)

Read Isaiah 6:8.
16) Describe Isaiah's response to God's question.

17) Compare Isaiah's response in verse 8 to his response in verse 5. What's the difference?

▪ Putting Feet to It

18) How can a God-perspective change your view of the challenges you face in life today?

19) What if you got a vision of God's greatness, plus His mercy and forgiveness during worship? How might that change your outlook on your future?

▪ Taking it With You

Matthew 16:16: "Simon Peter answered, 'You are the Christ, the Son of the living God.'" (NASB)

■ Journal

four
Worship
DEVELOPING OUR CHARACTER THROUGH WORSHIP
How worship helps us grow as followers of Jesus

Have nothing to do with godless myths and old wives' tales; rather, train yourself to be godly. For physical training is of some value, but godliness has value for all things, holding promise for both the present life and the life to come.

1 Timothy 4:7-8

Worship is to be a lifestyle. It's more than something we do for 20 minutes on Sunday morning. It's more than singing songs. We were created to worship God with our whole hearts and our entire lives. That means it's more than an experience—worship is our response to a loving and holy God.

Every day we respond to something or someone. We respond with our emotions, such as with joy when a loved one accepts Jesus as their Lord. We might respond with annoyance when someone cuts us off in traffic, or with sadness when someone we trust betrays us. We also respond with actions. We can respond with a cold shoulder when someone offends us, or with a gracious smile when someone accidentally spills our coffee. Our responses take many forms, but we respond every day.

To experience worship as a lifestyle, we should desire our responses to be more like Jesus. This involves a daily choice to align our thoughts and behavior to the character of Christ. Worship as a lifestyle means focusing first on our internal character, then our external actions. It means pursuing godliness as a way of life.

Character is somewhat hard to define. It's sort of our internal make up—a combination of our moral and ethical thoughts, actions, and reactions. Our character is who we really are when no one is looking. For a Christian, the standard for our character is very high. We serve a holy God who loves what is right, good, and true. We also serve a God who looks past our outward behavior and sees the truth of our character.

We have a saying at our church: Time and truth go hand in hand. God already knows our true character, and others will discover it with time. Before that sends you running for the back door, there is good news: Through worship, God can change our character!

When we worship or respond to God in all parts of our life, we see the fruits of a more godly character. When we worship God with our finances, we gain compassion for the poor. When we worship God with our time, we learn to sacrifice other things for God. When we worship God with our thoughts, we learn to submit and to trust. When we worship with our whole bodies (such as lifting our hands), we learn to seek the approval of God more than man.

One way worship develops our character is through the discipline it takes to worship in spirit and truth. When we discipline our thoughts and our time, we start to see our character being refined. Worship also helps us grow in other ways as a Christian. Without our response to God and our experience of God on a regular basis through worship, Christianity becomes dry. When our faith becomes dry, it's easy to give up or become unloving and legalistic. So, not only do we get to enjoy sweet fellowship with God in worship, we get to become more like Him. What a great promise!

■ Let's Talk

1) What are the character virtues you admire most in others?

2) If you could improve one aspect of your character, what would it be? Why is that important to you?

■ Entering In

Read Romans 12:1-2.

BytheWay ...

In the Old Testament, the Jews were accustomed to revolving their days around responding to God. There were feasts, offerings, meetings, and times of prayer. All of these responses were worship. So when Paul says, "I urge you ..." They said, "Oh, you mean do for Jesus some of the same kinds of things we've been doing as Jews?" For the Jewish people, worship was their lifestyle. They already knew how to worship; they just redirected the focus of their worship onto Jesus.

3) In the Old Testament, offering something as a sacrifice meant killing it. What do you think it means to offer our bodies as a "living" sacrifice?

4) How does sacrifice help develop godly character?

5) How does Romans 12:1-2 change the way you think about true worship?

6) Have you ever made anything from a pattern or a set of instructions? When we follow the instructions correctly, we know what the product will be. What happens when we conform to the pattern of this world? What will the product in our lives be?

7) What do these verses say is the key to knowing God's will in our lives?

8) How does worship renew our minds?

Read Hebrews 13:15.
9) When is it easiest to praise God?

10) Why is worshiping God sometimes a sacrifice?

11) What are some things we sacrifice to worship?

12) Praise is called the "fruit of lips that confess his name." Consider this phrase for a moment. Now consider the command to "continually" offer a sacrifice of praise. How might that impact the words we say?

Read Acts 2:42-47.

─────────────── **BytheWay ...** ───────────────
Acts chapter 2 shows us a beautiful picture of how the early Christians worshiped God with their lives. They show their character in how they devoted themselves to teaching, to fellowship, to sharing food together, prayer, and worship.

13) After reading these verses, what character traits do you see in the first Christians?

14) The Christian life isn't all about sacrifice. What are the benefits to individuals we see in this passage, or in our personal lives, when Christians choose to follow after Jesus and develop godly character through daily worship?

▪ Putting Feet to It

15) In Luke 6:46 Jesus says, "Why do you call me 'Lord, Lord' and do not do what I say?" It's so easy to call Jesus "Lord" during worship, then go our own way. How does your character need to change to truly worship Jesus as your Lord in all areas of your life?

16) If you are offering your body daily as a living sacrifice—as your spiritual act of worship—what changes might you have to make in your schedule, in your habits, and in your day-to-day choices?

▪ Taking It with You

Acts 2:42: "They were continually devoting themselves to the apostles' teaching and to fellowship, to the breaking of bread and to prayer." (NASB)

Journal

five
Worship
OVERCOMING HINDRANCES TO WORSHIP

How to press through obstacles to enter into God's presence

Let them praise his name with dancing and make music to him with tambourine and harp.

Psalm 149:3

One challenge to experiencing God fully in worship is that, for the most part, in the Western world, intimacy with the Lord is not valued, nor is it modeled. It's not a "cool" thing to do. Some people think (especially men) it makes them appear less macho or undignified to express emotion to God during worship. We're worried what other people will think about us. Not appearing weird is a high value for many of us.

Being constrained with our emotions toward the Lord is an unfortunate hang-up to have because God wants us to show Him our love. Throughout the Bible, when God's people worshiped Him, when they turned to kiss His face, they were very intimate, very demonstrative, and showed a lot of emotion. They would dance, clap, kneel, prostrate themselves, or shout loudly to the Lord.

You really can't turn toward to kiss the face of God will all of your heart, soul, and mind without at least occasionally showing emotion. We have to break through our "fear of man" and our culturally ingrained habit of restraining our emotions. Just because it's cultural does not mean it's biblical. God wants us to be intimate with Him, and at times that involves expressing what's happening in our hearts.

Overcoming the embarrassment of showing emotion is just one hindrance of worshiping God with our whole hearts. Satan knows that the Kingdom of God is advanced in mighty ways when we unite our hearts in worship. Consequently, he will work against each of us in different ways to discourage us from worshiping. He finds our weak points and digs in a foothold to stop us from offering ourselves in worship.

Do you tend to be judgmental? Then expect to have critical thoughts enter your mind about the band during worship. Do you struggle with being late? Then expect to lose your keys on Sunday morning. Are you worried about what others will think? Then you'll probably be inhibited in your experience of worship. Every one of us has weak points that our enemy exploits. Our job is to identify them and ask God to strengthen our vulnerable spots so we can worship freely.

Worship is a powerful part of our Christian life. Nothing should stand in the way of becoming worshipers of God. Although there are many more hindrances to worship, we are addressing three in this study: 1) the fear of man, 2) false worship, and 3) religion vs. relationship. We pray this study breaks down some of the walls that have kept you from responding to God wholeheartedly in worship.

■ Let's Talk

1) Think of a time you were so emotionally wound up about something that you shouted with joy or jumped up and down with excitement. Describe the experience and emotions you felt.

2) Have you ever held back from showing emotion because you were embarrassed? Describe.

Entering In

Read Proverbs 29:25.
3) How does the fear of man hinder our worship?

BytheWay ...

1 Chronicles 16 talks about David, the King of Israel. The Bible says David was a man after God's own heart. It's not that he was free from sin, but he was quick to repent of his sin. David also was not afraid to show his love for God in exuberant ways. This was especially true after he captured the Ark of the Covenant from the Philistines. As he brought the Ark back toward Jerusalem, he danced with joy in the streets wearing a linen ephod (a sleeveless tunic about hip length), a far cry from his normal kingly attire!

Read 2 Samuel 6:14-23.
4) Describe the scene in verses 14 and 15. What are some of the ways people are rejoicing and worshiping God?

5) In verses 16 and 20, Michal (David's wife and the daughter of the previous king, Saul) was watching the scene from a window. What was her response to David's display of emotion? What are some reasons she would respond like this?

6) In verse 21, David sets the record straight. What is his answer to Michal's complaints about his behavior?

7) How can David's answer help us with overcoming the fear of other's opinions?

Read Matthew 6:5-8.

BytheWay ...

Jesus tells us to not be like the hypocrites who pray to attract attention. The Greek word for "hypocrite" means play-actor. In this passage it refers to those who show fake piety.

---

8) Although this teaching by Jesus is about prayer, there is an obvious application for worship. How do we sometimes "fake" worship?

Five: Overcoming Hindrances to Worship

9) Jesus isn't telling His listeners to never pray out loud. Instead He's getting to the heart of the matter. What is Jesus really saying?

10) When "we go through the motions" of worship or do something to impress someone else, what is our reward going to be? (Read Matthew 6:1 for additional insight.)

11) What are some ways we can avoid falling into the trap of false worship?

──────────── **BytheWay ...** ────────────
In Mark 7, the Pharisees were once again trying to trap Jesus and prove Him wrong. The rule for the Pharisees and all the Jews was not to eat unless they had given their hands a ceremonial washing. This was a tradition, not something God asked them to do.

Read Mark 7:5-9.
12) In verses 6-8, Jesus quotes from the prophet Isaiah. What does Jesus say is the problem with the Pharisees?

13) Jesus clearly contrasts the commands of God and the tradition of men. How can we tell them apart?

14) Identify some human traditions that have become a hindrance to biblical worship.

Read Matthew 22:34-40.
15) Here's another example of the Pharisees trying to trap Jesus. This time they asked for the greatest commandment in the law. What was Jesus' answer?

16) How does Jesus' answer impact you today in regard to overcoming hindrances to worship?

BytheWay ...

If you have trouble telling God you love Him, perhaps it might help if you pictured Him as the Bible describes Him. For some mental images read Revelation 1:12-16, Revelation 4:2-7, Daniel 7:9-10 or Daniel 10:5-6.

■ Putting Feet to It

BytheWay ...

To overcome any hindrance to worship in our lives, we must be gut level honest about our own thoughts about how others worship. If you have experienced any judgmental thoughts about others, confess those and ask for forgiveness.

17) What are some reasons you have held back from showing emotion in worship?

18) What is one thing you can do this week to overcome a hindrance in your life to worship?

■ Taking It with You

Proverbs 29:25: "The fear of man brings a snare, But he who trusts in the Lord will be exalted." (NASB)

Journal

six
Worship
ADVANCING GOD'S KINGDOM THROUGH WORSHIP

How worship empowers us to do the works of Jesus

"Then I heard a loud voice in heaven say: 'Now have come the salvation and the power and the kingdom of our God, and the authority of his Christ. For the accuser of our brothers, who accuses them before our God day and night, they overcame him by the blood of the Lamb and by the word of their testimony ...'"
Revelation 12:11

In worship we acknowledge the lordship of Christ in our lives, we experience God with intimacy, He develops our character, and we gain a new perspective on life. Those would be incredible benefits on their own—but there's more.

In addition to deepening our personal faith, worship actively furthers the Kingdom of God. Amazing things happen when we worship: God overcomes our enemies, He empowers us to battle the forces of evil, we are strengthened to do good works, we spur one another on to good deeds, and God draws people to Himself. Worship isn't just about telling God how wonderful He is, it's also giving Him free reign to work through us and in us to advance His Kingdom.

The Psalms model a unique mix of praise and prayers. The psalmist many times alternately worships and adores God, then calls on Him for help and action. Psalm 74 records these words: "But you, O God, are my king from of old, you bring salvation upon the earth (v. 12). Then just a few verses later, the author writes, "Rise up, O God, and defend your cause …" (v. 22). The writer lists God's attributes, and then pleads for God to move on his behalf.

We also see evidence that God answers the pleas for help. Psalm 91:14 records, "'Because he loves me,' says the Lord, 'I will rescue him; I will protect him for he acknowledges my name.'" Our Old Testament ancestors knew that worship consisted of more than telling God He is worthy. Worship was their response to God about everything—to their helplessness, their hunger, and their lack of hope. In worship, they acknowledged God's power, called on God's power, then thanked Him for using His power to protect them.

God's Word shows He is ready and anxious to act on our behalf, but most times He waits for us to ask. While many of us may be comfortable asking God for help only in prayer, the Scriptures show that many times God responded to calls for help either during or as a result of worship. Could it be that God waits for us to acknowledge our need for Him in worship? Perhaps it's because when we worship and magnify God, He becomes greater as we become less. Or maybe it's like Jesus said, "My grace is sufficient for you, for my power is made perfect in weakness" (2 Corinthians 12:9). To some, worship seems like a "weak" way to accomplish important tasks, but to God it's a mighty weapon.

In this lesson we'll take a look at some of the ways in which God works through worship—not only in our lives, but in the lives of others.

■ Let's Talk

1) If you had all the power in the universe, identify a few things you would do to make this world a better place.

2) If you could personally do something for God and you knew you wouldn't fail, what would it be?

■ Entering In

BytheWay ...

This session's first Scripture reading is long, but it's an important story regarding how God moved on His people's behalf while they worshiped. Jehoshaphat was king of Judah, and his people were being attacked by an army significantly larger than theirs. Jehoshaphat knew they had no hope on their own to survive an attack. In desperation, he called his people to fast and turn their eyes to the Lord. What happened next is a miracle.

Read 2 Chronicles 20:1-30.
3) Look again at Jehoshaphat's prayer in verses five through 12. He speaks to God very personally. What are some of the things Jehoshaphat says to God to enlist His help against the enemy?

4) The people of Judah were in what looked like a hopeless situation. What are some common responses when our situations look hopeless?

5) Instead of building a wall to protect themselves or running away, what do the people do?

BytheWay ...

Fasting is an act of worship. Fasting is the practice of abstaining from food and sometimes drink for a given period of time (from 1 meal up to 40 days). Fasting was sometimes done to seek God in a greater manner, and can be done by individuals or groups, like we see in 2 Chronicles 20.

---

6) When God has the people's full attention, He sends a message through Jahaziel. What is the message?

7) Why would God make our enemies His enemies?

8) Through Jahaziel, the people of Judah are given specific instructions on where to stand the next morning. When they stand firm in their positions, what will God show them?

Six: Advancing God's Kingdom through Worship   55

9) The morning of battle, Jehoshaphat requests that some of the people start worshiping God. While they are singing and praising God, what happens?

10) Consider all the pieces of this story, especially the timing of the morning of battle. What applications can you make for yourself in your life?

Read Hebrews 10: 24-25.
11) These verses encourage Christians to continue meeting together. For what purposes?

12) Why would meeting together to worship and learn help Christians encourage each other?

13) What are some ways you can encourage your brothers and sisters in Christ that will advance the Kingdom of God?

ByTheWay ...

Psalm 22:3 tells us that God is "enthroned," or dwells, in the praises of His people. Psalm 91:9 promises, "If you make the Most High your dwelling," then God will "command his angels concerning you to guard you in all your ways" (v. 11).

Read Psalm 22:3 and Psalm 91.
14) Consider these two passages in light of each other. What is the relationship between worship and God acting on our behalf?

15) What are some ways we can make God our dwelling place?

■ Putting Feet to It

16) What are your most compelling reasons for worshiping God?

17) God wants to advance and expand His kingdom here on earth through men and women who will worship Him. What are some ways God might use you?

■ Taking It with You

Hebrews 10:24-25: "And let us consider how to stimulate one another to love and good deeds, not forsaking our own assembling together, as is the habit of some, but encouraging one another; and all the more as you see the day drawing near." (NASB)

Journal

leader's guide

one

SETTLING THE ISSUE OF LORDSHIP

Questions One and Two

The opening questions are designed to encourage members of the group to think about what drives them to make most of their decisions. These questions should start them thinking about what's important and, ultimately, what comes first in their lives. We can often tell what's important to us by looking at our calendar and our checkbook. These two paper trails record how we invest our time and money—is it on things of eternal value or things that will soon pass away? These questions will prepare the group to think about who or what is really Lord of their lives.

Question Three

In Exodus 19, we have a picture of the Israelites preparing to hear from God. Based on God's instructions in Exodus 19:10, the people are consecrating themselves on the outside to hear from God. This consecration was an outward act to symbolize an inward setting apart. God had chosen the Israelites to be His people and wanted them to be different on the outside and inside. This request by God demonstrates His desire for us to separate ourselves from our daily routine when we approach Him. We also learn that as the people waited at camp at the base of the mountain for God to appear, they trembled in fear as thunder and lightning came and a loud trumpet blast sounded. This sets the scene for God's words to be delivered to His people.

God first identifies Himself as their Lord. This is an important reminder of the covenant God made with their ancestor Abraham in Genesis 17. God then offers another reminder, this time of His faithfulness to the Israelites. This also serves to remind the people of God's graciousness, which is the foundation of the commandments He is about to give.

Questions Four and Five

At a first reading of Exodus 20:3, we might think serving other gods isn't a problem for us today. We dismiss this commandment as only for the Israelites who lived among people who made sacrifices to and worshipped pagan gods. Most Christians can't imagine having another god above the Lord. Encourage your group to look beyond the words and seek God's heart about this commandment. It is very easy to offer sacrifices or give honor to someone or something besides God. We choose to spend our time watching television instead of reading the Bible. We take an entire day to clean house, but neglect to honor the Sabbath. God's call to make Him first is one we should consider very seriously.

Here's what John Wesley wrote in "Wesley's Explanatory Notes" about the first commandment: "The sin against this commandment, which we are most in danger of, is giving that glory to any creature which is due to God only. Pride makes a God of ourselves, covetousness makes a God of money, sensuality makes a God of the belly. Whatever is loved, feared, delighted in, or depended on, more than God, that we make a god of." Although written in the mid-1700s, Wesley's observations still ring true today.

Question Six

God's commandments are always to benefit and protect us. When God commanded us to worship Him first, it was to save us from giving our lives to something false. Worshiping anything other than God opens us up to Satan's influence. Satan starts speaking lies into our hearts and leads us away from the truth. God created us and created this world. This means He knows best how things should work. When God is first in every part of our lives, and we are submitting to His will, then God is able to fulfill His plan for our lives—which is to bring about good.

In Matthew 6:33 Jesus said, "But seek first his kingdom and his righteousness, and all these things will be given to you as well." Jesus was reminding us to seek God first and to trust Him to take care of the rest.

Leader's Guide: Lesson One

Question Seven

An idol is anything or anyone we value more than God. It can even be a good thing. In biblical times, idols were things people could see and touch, and were often made of metal. In today's society most of our idols are not metal images, but mental images of what we want. Television is a source of many of those images. We see idols such as success, wealth, status, sensuality, and power. There were three primary idols in Bible times: Baal the god of sex and fertility, Mammon the god of money, and Molech the god of violence. It's interesting to note that people serve the same gods today, just in different forms.

Question Eight

Idols will always disappoint us because they are based on falsehood, and can never deliver what they promise. Jeremiah 10:11-14 describes their danger:

These gods, who did not make the heavens and the earth, will perish from the earth and from under the heavens. But God made the earth by his power; he founded the world by his wisdom and stretched out the heavens by his understanding. When he thunders, the waters in the heavens roar; he makes clouds rise from the ends of the earth. He sends lightning with the rain and brings out the wind from his storehouses. Everyone is senseless and without knowledge; every goldsmith is shamed by his idols. His images are a fraud; they have no breath in them."

Questions Nine and Ten

Idols lead us away from God. When something takes the place in our lives where God ought to be, we lose perspective. We seek after the image of something false and, in turn, lose what is real. For example, we seek a fantasy relationship that can ruin our marriage. We seek the status of wealth and can lose our integrity. Idols will always control us as we chase their lies. Psalm 115 describes these empty idols. They look good on the outside but are empty and worthless. When we chase after idols, we are in danger of becoming empty on the inside as well.

Question Eleven

In Roman 12:1 Paul refers to offering our bodies as living sacrifices. This might seem like a contradiction to submitting our wills. Does this mean we can submit our bodies but not our hearts? Not quite. The Jewish, or Hebraic, belief was that humans are a complete unit—not separating the body and spirit. When we submit to the Lordship of God in our lives, our entire being is involved.

When we acknowledge that Jesus is our Lord, Christianity is no longer something we do on Sunday or in our spare time. It's like dissolving Hershey's syrup into a glass of milk: the chocolate can either settle to the bottom (only affecting part of the milk), or it can be stirred throughout the milk and affect every part of it. That is what God wants from us! When Jesus is Lord over every part of our lives, we experience the richness of Christian living and we are pleased to offer ourselves, our whole selves, as a living sacrifice.

Whereas the pagan worshipers made sacrifices in order to get something they wanted, true worshipers offer themselves as a sacrifice in loving response for all God has done.

Questions Twelve and Thirteen

The final questions lead the participants to make a decision about who will be Lord of their lives. Depending upon the nature of your group, the answer to this last question may be one the members would like to keep to themselves. Some may not be ready to make God number one in their lives and will need to consider this further. Others may realize their need to make drastic changes in their hearts and lives. We encourage you to make your group a comfortable place for both seekers and those who are radically committed to Christ.

If you have members who are ready to make a first-time commitment to Jesus, then allow for some private time of prayer if needed. Your compassion and presence can encourage them to open up to what God wants to do in their lives.

two

EXPERIENCING GOD IN WORSHIP

Questions One and Two

Experiencing intimacy with God may be an uncomfortable topic for some people, especially new Christians. However, it's important that we understand worship isn't something weird or only for those spiritual "giants" of the faith. Worshiping God is as easy and natural as telling someone you love him or her.

Many Christians don't have a close relationship with God because they don't see Him has a person they can actually talk to. Learning to worship opens the door for a closer, more intimate relationship with our Heavenly Father.

Question Three

In the book of Leviticus, chapter 16, we read about the lengths to which the priests went to enter the presence of God. They did this in order to make atonement for the sins of all the Israelites. If the correct preparations weren't taken, the priests would die. The preparations for entering the Holy of Holies, where the Ark of the Covenant was kept and God's presence dwelt, included a special way of bathing, dressing, and of particular sacrifices. After making the sacrifices, the priest would put incense in hot coals to create a smoke screen as an additional protective covering.

Leviticus 16 also tells us of the practice of sending the sins of the people away on a scapegoat. Verses 21 and 22 describe the actions of the priest:

"Then Aaron shall lay both of his hands on the head of the live goat, and confess over it all the iniquities of the sons of Israel and all their transgressions in regard to all their sins; and he shall lay them on the head of the goat and send it away into the wilderness by the hand of a man who stands in readiness. The goat shall bear on itself all their iniquities to a solitary land; and he shall release the goat in the wilderness" (Leviticus 16:21-22).

This act symbolized the transfer of sin that we now experience through our union with Jesus Christ. Approaching God required a sacrifice. It's through Jesus Christ, and His sacrifice, that we now have access to the presence of God in heaven.

Question Four

Imagine the fear of the early Jewish believers. It had been ingrained in them since birth that only the priests were allowed to approach God, and if they made a mistake, it could mean their death. They must have needed much reassurance that it was now possible for the common man or woman to enter into the presence of God. Thus, the writer of the book of Hebrews (writing directly to the Jewish Christians) took great care to explain why they could now experience God for themselves.

Hebrews 4:8 tells the reader that Jesus, the Son of God, is now their high priest who opens the access door to God. Verses 15 and 16 of that same chapter go on to explain, "For we do not have a high priest who cannot sympathize with our weaknesses, but One who has been tempted in all things as we are, yet without sin. Therefore let us draw near with confidence to the throne of grace, so that we may receive mercy and find grace to help in time of need."

It's possible that many people still believe that God is unknowable. There is a false belief that God is too busy to be approached, or doesn't care about the "little" people. And yet the Scriptures tell us otherwise. This is an important truth for Christians to accept. God wants us to approach Him and know Him.

Question Five

It is an amazing truth that we can approach the God of the universe. Through the perfect sacrifice of the perfect priest, we can draw near to God with assurance. We did not earn this right. We cannot offer any sacrifice that would make us worthy to enter the "holy place" of God. It is only through the blood of Jesus that we are forgiven and cleansed from our sins. Hebrews 10:14 says, "because by one sacrifice he has made perfect forever those who are being made holy." This means us. "Being made holy" means being set apart by God for His purposes. That is God's will for every Christian—that our life would revolve around God's plan and purposes for us, and not our own.

Question Six

The "heart" stands for our whole inner life. God does not desire our empty worship; instead, He desires for us to present our entire selves to Him. In presenting ourselves to God, we must search our hearts and confess any wrongs. This is done with a sincere heart that longs to be pure before God. As we do that, we must know that it is only through faith that we receive forgiveness and an invitation to know God. There is such a tendency for us to want to please God with our actions. This verse reminds us that our confidence in approaching God is based on nothing we have done, but what He has done for us. This is great news for those who feel unworthy to approach God.

Question Seven

James 4:8 is set in a chapter where James is identifying some of the human practices and attitudes that drive us away from God. James' exhortation depicts a selfishness that causes divisions among fellow Christians, and a desire for worldly things. James calls the readers to humble themselves and submit to God, then issues the command to "come near" to Him. This is a call to repentance, which is given to us today. Yet even though we are called to repent, James assures us when we turn to God He is ready to turn to us.

Jesus illustrated God's heart to turn to us when we turn to Him in the Parable of the Prodigal Son. When the son repents of his selfish ways and turns to return home to his father, the father is anxiously waiting for him. Luke 15 gives us these words of Jesus:

"But while he was still a long way off, his father saw him and was filled with compassion for him; he ran to his son, threw his arms around him and kissed him. The son said to him, 'Father, I have sinned against heaven and against you. I am no longer worthy to be called your son.' But the father said to his servants, 'Quick! Bring the best robe and put it on him. Put a ring on his finger and sandals on his feet. Bring the fattened calf and kill it. Let's have a feast and celebrate. For this son of mine was dead and is alive again; he was lost and is found.' So they began to celebrate" (Luke 15: 20b-24).

God's response is lavish and depicts grace, when we fulfill our part to "turn." In worship we turn from our preoccupation with daily concerns, we turn from our self-focus, we turn from judgmental thoughts of how badly the band is playing or the choir is singing, or how someone is dressed. We turn from anything that keeps us from opening our hearts fully to God and knowing Him more.

Question Eight

The NIV Bible Commentary makes this observation about James 4:8:

"The call to 'wash your hands' is a command to make one's conduct pure. Similarly, the call to 'purify your hearts' insists on purity of thoughts and motives."

When we seek pleasure and self-gratification, we can often find ourselves in the wrong place, doing the wrong things, with the wrong thoughts. It is consistent with James' call to humble ourselves that we do a self-review and confess any sin before coming to God in worship. The psalmist gave us a beautiful prayer that might help as we prepare ourselves for worship:

"Search me, O God, and know my heart; try me and know my anxious thoughts, and see if there be any hurtful way in me, and lead me in the everlasting way" (Psalm 139:23-24, NASB).

Questions Ten and Eleven

There is a term theologians use to describe the manifest presence of God. It is called the "pneumas" of God. That means God's presence comes and fills a particular geographical location. When we worship God, He comes and "sits down" among us and we experience His manifest presence—His "pneumas."

Questions Thirteen and Fourteen

For hundred of years, Christians have sung beautiful hymns of worship recounting the goodness and majesty of God. These songs are wonderful songs about God. Many of today's worships songs also speak of God's wonder and majesty, but are sung to God.

It's important to sing and speak of the greatness of God, and His mighty deeds. However, only singing about God doesn't deepen our relationship with Him. Just as talking about your friend isn't the same as talking directly to her. But when we sing directly to Him, we open up the line of communication and can experience God more personally and intimately.

The Psalms are filled with words of love, adoration, pain and pleading—many directed to God. David poured out his heart to the God he loved. Despite all of David's personal weakness and sin, God still named him a man after His own heart. David humbled himself, repented of his sins and dove in deep to experience all God had to offer.

Questions Fifteen and Sixteen

It takes preparation to fully experience God in worship. We can't run into church late, sing a few songs and expect God to show up, or expect to experience God in a deep way. To experience God in worship, we should make every effort to be spiritually, physically and emotionally ready. That doesn't mean putting on a happy face. It means being honest with ourselves and with God about where our hearts are.

It also means taking some practical steps to prepare ourselves to meet Him. Show up at church early. Allow time to read through the bulletin, greet a few friends, and then sit down and willingly refocus your attention on God. Discipline your thoughts and spend time in personal reflection. It's not always easy, depending on what our morning or day has been like. But the reward we will receive is worth the self-discipline. God is anxiously waiting, just like the father in the Prodigal Son, for us to draw near to Him so He can draw near to us.

Leader Notes

# three

EXPERIENCING GOD IN WORSHIP

Questions One and Two

The first two questions are designed to stimulate thoughts about things or people that inspire us. What are some of their characteristics? This is a launching pad to consider how understanding God's awe-inspiring character can change our lives.

Question Three

You can imagine the rumors about who Jesus really was. The Jewish people had waited thousands of years for the promised Messiah. However, they expected someone grander than a humble carpenter. Some people thought Jesus was John the Baptist raised from the dead. That's an interesting thought since John actually baptized Jesus in the Jordan River and other people would have seen them together (Matthew 3:13-17, Luke 3:21). Sadly, John was beheaded by "Herod the tetrarch" for speaking out against Herod's immoral relations with his brother's wife.

Some thought Jesus was Elijah, an Old Testament prophet, and was a forerunner to the real Messiah yet to come. Elijah was foretold in Malachi 4:5-6 as a messenger: "See, I will send you the prophet Elijah before that great and dreadful day of the Lord comes. He will turn the hearts of the fathers to their children and the hearts of the children to their fathers; or else I will come and strike the land with a curse."

Yet others thought Jesus was Jeremiah come back to life. Jeremiah was another Old Testament prophet. It had been hundreds of years since the Jewish people had been sent a prophet and they were ready to hear from God.

Question Four

One thing we learn about Jesus' questions as He interacts with a variety of people in the New Testament is He already knows the answer. Jesus doesn't ask Peter this question—"Who do you say I am?"—for Jesus' benefit, but for Peter's. Many times God calls us to that same point of decision. He says, "You've called me friend, you've asked for My help with your job, you've cried out in your point of darkest need, but who do you really say that I am?" As we enter in to worship, this is a crucial question to answer in our own hearts. When we do so, we start to take on a God-perspective on life that helps us make sense of our troubles.

Question Five

Peter's answer that Jesus was the "Christ" reveals that he believed Jesus was the promised Messiah. This is a bold declaration after acknowledging that many thought Jesus was a forerunner to the Messiah. Christ is actually a title for Jesus. After the Resurrection, however, Christians started using it as part of Jesus' name—Jesus Christ.

Peter and the disciples were coming to a deeper understanding of the truth of who Jesus was, bit by bit. Not unlike us. As humans limited to earthly time and space, we struggle with understanding the whole truth of who Jesus really is. As our understanding grows, we grow in our faith and trust that He can handle any problem we have.

Question Six

Understanding who God is, and what He is able to do in our lives, enhances our God-perspective. God is not wringing His holy hands in heaven wondering how He's going to get us out of our latest mess. He has not given up on us, thinking we have no hope. Before we even ask for help, He has a plan to offer. And one of the best truths about God is that He will bring good out of the worst looking situation. Knowing this, we can worship with abandonment and faith, trusting Him to cover us with protection and mercy.

Question Seven

Some people in your group may struggle with understanding who God is. This can be confusing for someone new to church. We tend to use names for God interchangeably: Jesus, God, Holy Spirit, Father, and Son. Years ago, when I (Glynnis) was sharing my faith with my earthly father, I told him that God came to earth as a man, and that man was Jesus. He looked at me in surprise and said, "No one ever told me that. You mean Jesus and God are the same?" My dad had gone to church as a small boy and never understood this important fact.

Consider if this might be an opportunity to discuss in greater detail the concept of the Trinity, and why the fact that acknowledging Jesus is God is critically important. If you struggle with this concept yourself, speak with your pastor before your group meeting, or with a biblically knowledgeable individual. If you still feel unsure about how to explain the depth of God's personalities, consider inviting someone to speak at your small group.

In addition to this, Jesus' response to Peter gives hope that when our limited understanding is stretched, God will help us understand His immensity. "Blessed are you, Simon son of Jonah, for this was not revealed to you by man, but by my Father in heaven" (Matthew 16:17).

Question Eight

This is the only place in the Bible where seraphs are mentioned. The NIV Bible Commentary makes this observation: "The seraphs are bright creatures, for the word means 'burning ones'; yet they hide their faces from the greater brightness and the glory of the Lord. Covering the feet suggests humility."

Questions Nine and Ten

The seraphs repeat the word "holy" three times describing God. The early church leaders interpreted this passage in support of the doctrine of the trinity: God the Father, God the Son and God the Holy Spirit. We can incorporate this understanding, whether correctly interpreted or not, in our own worship of God. As we sing, "You are holy, holy, holy ...", we can honor God in His fullness.

Isaiah never forgets the vision he had of God's incredible glory. When we grasp God's glory in worship, we too never forget it. It draws us back to worship to experience it again and again. But it shouldn't stop there. Remembering God's holiness should change our everyday experience. It can give us confidence to step out of our comfort zone. It helps us battle the fear of man or the fear of the unknown. It can also keep us from sinning so that we don't disappoint such a righteous God.

Question Eleven

We can almost feel Isaiah's heart breaking over his sin. There's nothing God says to Isaiah to make him feel this way. Just a vision of God's holiness brings Isaiah to a point of repentance. Additionally, as we learned in lesson two, the Jews thought they would die if they saw God face to face. So, in addition to being humbled, Isaiah simply thought he was toast!

As we come to an understanding of who God is, our sin can seem even darker. Yet it is not God's desire that we are crushed by our sinfulness. Instead, God draws us to Himself with kindness (Romans 2:4). In light of that, we want to turn from our sin, accept His forgiveness and embrace all God has to offer.

Question Twelve

Scripture tells us two things about Satan: (1) He's the accuser of the brethren (Revelation 12: 10-11), and (2) He's the father of lies (John 8:44). Satan points his ugly finger at us and spouts lies like: "God will never forgive you," "God could never use someone like you," and "You have no future." These are harsh lies intended to set you on the sidelines of life and make you an ineffective Christian.

God, on the other hand, allows His light to shine on our sins in order to wash away the darkness in our souls. Romans 8:1-2 promises, "Therefore, there is now no condemnation for those who are in Christ Jesus, because through Christ Jesus the law of the Spirit of life set me free from the law of sin and death."

Question Fifteen

Romans chapter three offers the answer to the question of where our hope comes from:

Romans 3:21-24 says, "But now a righteousness from God,

apart from law, has been made known, to which the Law and the Prophets testify. This righteousness from God comes through faith in Jesus Christ to all who believe. There is no difference, for all have sinned and fall short of the glory of God, and are justified freely by his grace through the redemption that came by Christ Jesus."

Many of us try to become "righteous" based on our actions. We hope that somehow we can make up for the sins of our past. Yet, this passage in Romans makes it clear that we are justified (made "not guilty") through Jesus Christ.

Questions Sixteen and Seventeen

God's forgiveness made all the difference to Isaiah. In verse five we see a man humbled in the presence of a holy God. We even see a hint of despair. Yet when offered forgiveness, Isaiah is transformed into a man willing to go wherever God sends him. Isaiah responded with a ready "Yes, God" as a response to grace.

Worshiping God and serving Him go hand in hand. In 1 Chronicles 16:8-9 we read, "Give thanks to the Lord, call on his name; make known among the nations what he has done. Sing to him, sing praise to him; tell of all his wonderful acts." Not only are we filled with gratitude when we worship God, but God fills us with boldness to make Him known among people.

Questions Eighteen and Nineteen

Being in God's presence can change the way we look at all areas of our lives. As we get a vision of God's holiness and our need for Him, our perspective on life changes. In fact, it should change everything. We start to see the big picture and how we fit in. We see that our pain has a purpose. We see that we are needy, yet valued by the Creator of the universe. In worship we get our perspective of life turned upside down—it's not about us! It's all about God.

Leader Notes

four

EXPERIENCING GOD IN WORSHIP

Questions One and Two

Our character matters to God. We can put on the finest Christian act when "important" people are watching, but if we neglect to care for someone in need, then we displease God. It's easy to fool others into thinking we have godly character, but God knows the truth.

We see a picture of godly character in the person of Jesus Christ. As members of the group list the character virtues they admire most, you'll see them modeled in the life of Jesus, such as compassion, kindness, love, patience, graciousness, and forgiveness. These are just a few of the character traits of Christ.

Question Three

We often see ourselves as very fortunate spiritually to be living during this time. There are many advantages, but there are disadvantages too. One is that we are thousands of years, a continent, and many generations removed from the life and times of Jesus as a human being. So when Paul makes his statement about being a living sacrifice, it has to be understood with the knowledge of the sacrificial system. Paul's hearers knew what he meant. They could bring a vivid picture to their minds of a lamb being slaughtered on the altar. With that illustration, they understood the complete sacrifice God asked of them.

We are trained that we give our heart to Jesus when we are born again; but we oftentimes think we can offer the rest of us later, when we want to. That's why some Christians have a hard time even giving up a few hours of time to meet together or giving from the first fruits of their income to God.

Spend some time with your group being very practical about what our Christian lives would look like if we offered all our lives as a sacrifice.

Question Four

A sacrifice denotes doing something that costs us. And part of that is choosing to worship and praise God even when we don't feel like it, when we don't feel His presence, or when our circumstances are difficult. We might be in pain or experiencing grief, and worshiping God is the last thing we want to do. In these circumstances, we learn the discipline of preparing to worship and then worshiping. We learn to override our selfish thoughts to do what is right. We learn to take our thoughts captive to the obedience of Christ (2 Corinthians 10:5). As we learn to discipline our thoughts and actions in relation to worship, that overflows into other areas of our lives.

Helen Keller wrote these words about character: "Character cannot be developed in ease and quiet. Only through experience of trial and suffering can the soul be strengthened, vision cleared, ambition inspired, and success achieved."

Because we are naturally self-focused, offering our lives as a sacrifice to God will likely mean we'll suffer. But the rewards of a more godly character will be worth it in the long run.

Question Five

This passage in Romans makes it clear that worship is something we do every day and everywhere. In the past, the people of God presented sacrifices and worshiped at the altar in the temple. Today, our altar is everywhere, and we don't have to wait for a particular day to worship God.

Also, we learn that worship involves our whole being. A sacrifice was acceptable only when the animal was offered completely. You wouldn't cook yourself some lamb chops for dinner and offer the rest of the animal as your sacrifice the next day! A sacrifice involved every part of the animal. To be living sacrifices means we are to offer ourselves completely. Everything that is done by our bodies—what we think, do, and say—can be an act of spiritual worship if it is done as an offering to God.

It's so easy to sacrifice, or offer, only parts of ourselves to God. We may say, "God, you can have the words that come out of my mouth, but I want to keep what I see with my eyes." Our goal as believers is to be maturing towards submitting every part of our lives to God as a sacrifice.

Question Six

Our pattern of living as Christians is the life of Jesus. Romans 8:29 says, "For those God foreknew he also predestined to be conformed to the likeness of his Son, that he might be the firstborn among many brothers." When we pattern our lives after what we see in the world, we end up with a product that's hollow, shallow, and short-lived. But when we use the life of Jesus as our pattern, we end up with true joy, peace that passes understanding, and everlasting love.

Question Seven

Verse one helps us understand verse two. When we dedicate our lives as living sacrifices to God, our minds are transformed through acts of worship. As our minds are transformed, and our character is changing to be more like Christ, we will naturally choose to do things that are in line with God's will for us. It will be our heart's desire to serve God, and that in itself is part of God's will for us.

This transformation occurs over time as we are "renewing" our mind. This tense implies an ongoing process, not something that happens once.

Question Eight

When we choose to worship, we discipline our thoughts toward things of God, things that are pure and righteous. As we do that, we develop the habit of thinking right thoughts, and from right thoughts flow right actions.

Disciplining our thoughts takes practice. At first, we might only be able to focus our minds on God for a few minutes. Don't be discouraged if that's all you can manage. As with any type of discipline, mastery comes over time. You wouldn't start lifting weights and expect to bench press 300 pounds in a week. Nor would you expect to be able to sit down at the piano and play a concerto in a month.

If you are new to worshiping God, expect to continually pull your thoughts back to where they should be. Don't be hard on yourself; just keep persevering. Over time, you'll find it easier to concentrate on God; and when that happens, you'll find your mind being renewed in supernatural ways.

Question Nine

In this fallen world, we can experience tragedy and loss that bring us to our knees. It's a human response to wonder how a good God could allow such horrible things to happen. Certainly, we think, God could have—no, should have—intervened! We can sometimes question God's love for us and His faithfulness.

In times like that, it is a sacrifice of our will and emotions to worship God. Everything in us may want to shake our fist at Him and turn away. If we have developed our character, and persevered in the discipline of worship, we will choose to deny our flesh and enter into worship. As we do so, we find that God meets us in our despair, and He starts to bring healing through the very thing we wanted to avoid.

Question Ten

Many years ago, before I was a pastor, I (Brian) decided that my preparation for worship on Sunday should start Saturday night. So, my wife and I made a commitment to God to go to bed early on Saturday night. There have been a few exceptions, but this involved many sacrifices of our social life. Another sacrifice we decided to make in order to worship God more fully was to get up early on Sunday morning. That way we had time to solve many of the normal Sunday morning problems—like not finding the right shoes, picking the right clothes, and having time for our devotions. Another decision we made was to get to church early. This gave us time to greet people and find a seat.

These may sound like simple things to do, but for many, these ideas will take some sacrifice. They did (and do) for us!

When we consider worship as our daily response to God, we will deal with many sacrifices of our will. Offering ourselves as a living sacrifice will go against our natural tendency. This is where a well-developed character comes in to play.

Question Eleven

The early Christians were filled with the Holy Spirit. Knowing this, we can imagine that these Christians were exhibiting the fruit of the Spirit outlined in Galatians 5:22-23:

"But the fruit of the Spirit is love, joy, peace, patience, kindness, goodness, faithfulness, gentleness and self-control. Against such things there is no law."

Question Fourteen

There's no denying that God's way seems opposite to man's way. God's math doesn't work like we think it should. How can 90 percent of our income go further than 100%? How can we put our earthly nature to death and then receive life? How can someone sell all their possessions, give to those in need, and have glad and sincere hearts? This is the part of God you have to experience to believe! Once you experience God's way, you realize it doesn't have to make sense! It just works.

Questions Fifteen and Sixteen

We should not take lightly the words we sing during worship. God takes them seriously, and so should we. We sing, "Who is like you, oh Lord?" We invite Him to "be the center" of our lives, and proclaim "be glorified in me." All these words mean something.

Unless we've disciplined our character, we will walk out of church as though nothing happened. But it has. We've sung words of love and commitment to a holy God. Our lives should reflect that commitment. Every day we are called to be a living sacrifice as our spiritual act of worship. Singing is one way we worship, but our daily choices and how we respond to God, are also our spiritual acts of worship.

Consider reviewing the words of some worship songs your church uses with your group. Think about these words as you discuss what types of changes you might have to make in your character, thought life, schedule, and habits to honor God.

Leader Notes

five

EXPERIENCING GOD IN WORSHIP

Questions One and Two

Not showing emotion in worship is a man-made cultural tradition—mainly in Western countries. However, it's completely acceptable in our culture to show great emotion at a ball game, concert, play, or movie—just not in church. Picture what football fans will do to cheer on their team: paint their faces green, put cheese hats on their heads, wear no shirts in freezing weather, and basically go wild (especially in front of the television camera).

For many reasons, we have decided it's acceptable to display emotion in some settings and not in others. We are comfortable around some people and not others. Unless we are very strong in our beliefs, being around judgmental people will hinder any display of emotion.

This could be a challenging session for some people, depending on what type of church background they have. As the leader, please be prayerfully prepared for disagreements. Graciously acknowledge everyone's opinions, yet always bring the discussion back to what the Bible has to say.

The bottom line is that only God knows the truth about what's going on inside our hearts. The quietest person might be praising God the most in his or her heart. And the most boisterous worshiper might ... well, you get the point. We are not to judge anyone, only seek to know about God's heart on worship through studying Scripture.

Question Three

We grow up seeking the approval of others—first our parents, then teachers, and then friends. It's a natural desire to want a "thumbs up" from those we respect and love. However, it becomes a snare when we seek the approval of others more than the approval of God.

We can easily use the approval of others as our measuring stick for how we are doing in all areas of our lives. We worry about how we look, how well we perform at sports, how well we do on our jobs, will the right people accept us into their group of friends, etc. When we do that, we start to define ourselves by what others think of us. That might be okay if we could depend on others to never change their opinions of us—but that won't happen. Friends will flake out, spouses sometimes leave, and kids may rebel.

Proverbs 29:25 reminds us that the only place to find true security is through trusting in the Lord. When we plant this truth deep in our hearts, we will find freedom in many places where we've previously been in bondage to the approval of others.

Question Five

Michal might have a number of reasons for despising David's show of emotion. As the daughter and then wife of a king, she probably had pre-determined opinions on how a king ought to act. Instead of basing those opinions on love, she based them on rules she had been taught by others or had worked up for herself.

In allowing her thoughts to be judgmental, Michal is displaying pride in her life. Psalm 18:27 gives us insight into God's opinion of her attitude: "You save the humble but bring low those whose eyes are haughty. If we want to experience God intimately in worship we need to ruthlessly eliminate any hint of pride in our own lives. Psalms 138:6 tells us why: "Though the Lord is on high, he looks upon the lowly, but the proud he knows from afar."

One hint that pride is lifting its ugly head is if you think in your mind, "I would never ..." Can't you almost hear Michal's thoughts? "I would never dance like that in public; what would the slave girls think?" Unless we are dealing with sin, that type of attitude sets us up for a fall. Who cares what anyone else thinks! David is a great example of someone in a position of respect and authority who openly sought God's approval more than man's. A wonderful thing about this story is that David retained all the respect he had from the people (except Michal and her father), and it even increased.

Question Six

Michal certainly intended her words to shame David into acting a different way. She tried to change David's style of worship by reminding him that he was king of Israel, and by suggesting that he was vulgar in what he chose to wear in front of slave girls.

David was confident. Not only in his position as king, but in his choice of how, when, and where to worship. David did not base his response to God on his personal philosophy of worship, nor did he defend his rights because he had attained his kingly position through strength or manipulation and could do what he wanted. David was confident because God appointed him as king, and it was David's joy to celebrate before his Lord.

Question Seven

One way to overcome the fear of man is to keep things in perspective. Ask yourself, "What's the worst thing that could happen?" Then ask yourself, "What's the worst thing that could happen if I succumb to the fear of man?" 2 Corinthians 5:9 is a great Scripture to help us keep our focus on what's important: "So we make it our goal to please him, whether we are at home in the body or away from it."

Question Nine

In chapter six, Jesus addresses three important components of faith: giving, prayer, and fasting. He assumes His listeners will continue giving, praying, and fasting—so these verses aren't "proof" not to give to the needy or pray out loud. Jesus is cautioning them about having right motives.

Worship is our personal response to God. If it takes any other form, such as to receive honor by man or so people will think we are super spiritual, then we are doing it for the wrong reasons. God longs for any response from us, so long as it is authentic.

Question Ten

God loves to reward His children. Often, those of us who are parents think that a "reward" is equivalent to a bribe. But that's not how God approaches the idea of rewards. Scripture tells us that

God is our reward (Genesis 15:1), God rewards for faithfulness (1 Samuel 26:23), children are a reward (Psalm 127:3), and that our eternal reward will be in heaven (Matthew 5:12).

Here is one of the first passages where we learn that we can also earn no reward. Jesus warns in Matthew 6:1: "Be careful not to do your 'acts of righteousness' before men, to be seen by them. If you do, you will have no reward from your Father in heaven."

Questions Twelve to Fourteen

Jesus knew that the Pharisees had fallen far away from the heart of God. It seemed they loved the law more than they loved God. The Pharisees had created an enormous number of rules about life that basically consisted of formality and legalism. Jesus minced no words about their hypocrisy. Matthew 23:26-28 records these words of Jesus:

"Blind Pharisee! First clean the inside of the cup and dish, and then the outside also will be clean. Woe to you, teachers of the law and Pharisees, you hypocrites! You are like whitewashed tombs, which look beautiful on the outside but on the inside are full of dead men's bones and everything unclean. In the same way, on the outside you appear to people as righteous but on the inside you are full of hypocrisy and wickedness."

Jesus felt even more strongly about their false worship and love of religion because they were supposed to be spiritual leaders for the people!

With this warning from Jesus, we need to take care to avoid becoming like the Pharisees. We need to be always pursuing a relationship with God over religious practices. We can easily fall into loving religion when we think that by only keeping the rules we are pleasing God. Many of the unwritten "rules" in churches today started with good intentions, but then tradition took over and made them "law." Some of these include what we wear to church, how we speak in church, and what we don't participate in outside of church.

Questions Fifteen and Sixteen

Jesus was always bringing the conversation back to our hearts.

The Pharisees had expanded the Law into 613 different commandments. Jesus summed the whole law up in one commandment, and then expanded it into two. Our soul can be described as our mind, emotions, and will. Our mind is our "thinker"; our emotions are our "feeler"; and our will is our "chooser." God made every part of us to worship Him. This applies to our intellect, our emotions, and our actions. Although we may lean towards worshiping God in a certain way, it's good to explore all ways. One thing we need to remember is worship always comes back to responding to God in love.

Questions Seventeen and Eighteen

Although we've addressed three common hindrances to worship, there are many more. Some people have never known the love of an earthly father, and therefore don't know how to respond to their Heavenly Father. Some people have been hurt by people or "religion" and don't trust anyone—especially with their emotions. Still others have grown up with disrespect for authority, and consequently struggle with submission. The only way to change is to honestly acknowledge where we are first. This may take time and prayer to get to the bottom of why someone struggles with worshiping God. Because it's one of our highest callings as believers, it's important to spend time assessing our personal hindrances to worship and addressing them, one by one, until we can worship freely.

Leader Notes

six

ADVANCING GOD'S KINGDOM THROUGH WORSHIP

Questions One and Two

It's fun to dream about how we would eliminate poverty, find a cure for cancer, or feed every hungry child if we could do "anything!" The purpose of these questions isn't to leave us day-dreaming, but to think about what God might actually like to do through us. The Bible is full of miracles God performed through ordinary people—they just had faith in an extraordinary God. Have we forgotten that God doesn't like poverty, hunger, or disease any more than we do?

These questions set the participant up to consider three different aspects of advancing the kingdom through worship—God acts when we worship; in worship we spur one another on to good deeds; and God protects us when we dwell in Him through worship. As with all the other sessions, these are just a few of the ways God advances His kingdom through worship. Perhaps your group can identify other scriptures and other ways God works in us and through us.

Question Three

Jehoshaphat uses a model of prayer that we can learn from when facing our own "impossible" situations. After fasting to show his sincerity, Jehoshaphat includes three different approaches.

First, he praises God for who He is now. He acknowledges that God is ruler over everything, and that power and might are in His hands.

Second, he praises God for what He has done, specifically how God handled similar problems. Jehoshaphat "reminds" God that He eliminated other threats in the past and provided the very land where the battle is about to take place.

Finally, Jehoshaphat admits that he and his people are hopeless with God. "For we have no power to face this vast army that is attacking us. We do not know what to do, but our eyes are upon you" (v. 12).

Question Four

One reason the force of the army was overwhelming was that it was a combined invasion of three different forces from Moab, Ammon, and Mount Seir. Perhaps Jehoshaphat and his men could have handled one army, but three armies were just too much. This can be a reason we get overwhelmed at times. We can handle one problem, but then two or three more pile on top—and we get crushed.

Another reason the advancing army might have been a threat was they took a little-used route and were attacking from the south. Any time a problem arises from a new direction, we can feel hopeless. This is particularly true when something or someone drastically changes.

When we are faced with hopeless and drastic situations, we respond in a variety of ways. A common first response is to try and figure out a human solution. If we are in debt, we borrow money. If we lose a job, we run out and buy a newspaper for the want ads. If someone hurts us, we self-medicate the pain. The more severe the situation, the more drastic the reaction.

Another response is to give up without trying. If we think we can avoid more pain, we will quit. Neither option gives God the opportunity to display His power.

Question Five

First, Jehoshaphat proclaimed a fast. Fasting makes no sense to the natural mind. How can not eating do anything besides make us irritable? We don't know exactly how it works, but fasting is one way God chooses to advance His kingdom here on earth—in our hearts and through our actions.

Fasting is an act of obedience and it humbles our soul before God. Galatians 6:7-9 says, "Do not be deceived, God is not mocked; for whatever a man sows, this he will also reap. For the one who sows to his own flesh will from the flesh reap corruption, but the one who sows to the Spirit will from the Spirit reap eternal life" (NASB). In fasting, we are denying our flesh and submitting to the Spirit of God. Jehoshaphat knew he had no human chance to deal with the impending threat in his own strength. If there was any hope to be found, it would be from God.

The next thing the Israelites did was gather together from every town in Judah "to seek help from the Lord" (v.4). The people gathered at what was their local "church"—"the temple of the Lord" (v. 5).

There are important dynamics which happen when we get together to seek the Lord. The faith of the strong buoys the faith of the weak. Plus, we can experience God's presence in a greater way. God wants us to gather regularly and be His body, so He withholds certain things from us as individuals that we can only experience as a group. Psalm 87:2 says, "The Lord loves the gates of Zion more than all the other dwelling places of Jacob" (NASB). The gates of Zion represent all of the tribes of Israel gathered together. God loves it when His children are gathered together even more than when we worship Him as individuals.

When we meet together to worship, the Lord is present in a special way. Jesus' words about this are recorded in Matthew 18:19-20: "Again, I tell you that if two of you on earth agree about anything you ask for, it will be done for you by my Father in heaven. For where two or three come together in my name, there am I with them."

After receiving the word from the Lord through Jahaziel, everyone fell down in worship before God. Through fasting, meeting together to seek God's face, and worshiping, God was preparing to act on His people's behalf.

Question Six

The Bible paints a beautiful picture of men, women, children, and babies standing side-by-side to seek help from God. They are waiting with expectancy for God to answer their prayers. They fully expect God to come, and they aren't disappointed.

In response, God gives His people words of encouragement, comfort, and hope. He reassures them that the battle is His, gives them the overview of the battle, and promises to be right there with them.

Question Seven

God is a loving father who protects His children. However, it's also true that when we are followers of God, it's actually His enemies who become ours—not the other way around. That's what God meant by "For the battle is not yours, but God's" (v. 15). This is spiritual warfare. Ephesians chapter 6 outlines the battle that Christians find themselves in because of our allegiance to Jesus Christ:

"Finally, be strong in the Lord and in his mighty power. Put on the full armor of God so that you can take your stand against the devil's schemes. For our struggle is not against flesh and blood, but against the rulers, against the authorities, against the powers of this dark world and against the spiritual forces of evil in the heavenly realms." (Ephesians 6:10-12)

The passage doesn't say to arm ourselves with weapons of this world, but to put on the "full armor of God" to do battle. We are given spiritual weapons that far surpass the efficiency of metal. Jehoshaphat and his army did just that—they employed spiritual weapons by putting on the armor of God through fasting, prayer, and worship. Although it was God's battle, they were still at risk. That's why God will go into battle on our behalf when we are in danger.

Question Eight

God promised that if the people put themselves in a position of faith and worship, He would let them see the direction the enemy was coming, and they would be able to watch while they were delivered.

The key here was the Israelites couldn't get into the battle. They were told to stand firm and face their enemies – but not defend themselves nor attack. There are many possibilities for why God would have had the Israelites watch the battle from a distance. One reason is that if they got involved, they could have taken partial or full credit for the victory. Since they had nothing to do with the actual battle, they knew it was completely God's doing and He got all the credit.

Sometimes this applies to our own lives. There are times when

God might not want us in the heat of battle. Sometimes the best place for us is to keep our eyes on God and watch Him deal with the issue. We can learn from Jehoshaphat to completely depend on God to give us direction as to when to fight and when to stand firm and watch our deliverance come from His hand. Plus, in every situation we can learn to worship God before we do anything else.

Question Nine

Before the people set out to position themselves to watch the battle, Jehoshaphat appointed men to lead the contingency and to sing praises while they were leading. The Scripture says "as" or, in other words, at the same time they were worshiping, the Lord set ambushes for the enemy. This frustrated the men of all three armies so that they attacked each other and completely annihilated themselves.

By the time the men of Judah got to their position, the battle was over and there were no survivors. Not only were God's people saved, but they gathered the plunder from the fallen men.

Question Ten

This important story has a variety of applications for our lives. A strong application for this study is how God uses worship to defeat the enemy and protect us. Spend time with your group exploring all the personal applications God shows to each of you.

Question Twelve

When we worship God and focus on His character, we get a greater ability to experience His heart. When this happens, we see that it is full of pure and unconditional love for His children. As we open our hearts to receive God's love, He often allows us to share in that love for others.

Occasionally, as I (Glynnis) have worshiped, I find myself in tears. Sometimes this is due to a sense of my own overwhelming love and thankfulness. But at other times, God breaks my heart over what breaks His—lost and hurting people. It's as if I can see others as God sees them.

When we see others with God's eyes, we can't help but love

them and want the best for them. In wanting the best for them, we long to help others achieve their God-given potential and help them fulfill all God has for them.

Question Thirteen

Every day men and women walk into our churches defeated from their past, their present, and their lack of hope for a future. As God starts to work in their lives and they learn the truth about their great value and God's purpose for their lives, the despair starts to lift. Christian brothers and sisters can help the healing process along.

Some ways we can help each other include being a godly example, telling the truth in love, teaching classes, leading small groups, affirming God's gifts and talents in each other, and supporting each other through hard times. Your small group is probably the best place for this to happen. Pray for God to show you ways to build each other up.

Romans 15:1-2 says, "We who are strong ought to bear with the failings of the weak and not to please ourselves. Each of us should please his neighbor for his good, to build him up."

Question Fourteen

The Psalms are filled with encouraging truths about God and His longing to act on our behalf. These two passages have an interesting tie-in with the concept of dwelling where God dwells. In Psalm 22:3 the word *enthroned* is "yashab" in Hebrew and means to dwell, remain or abide—God dwells in our worship! Then, in Psalm 91:1 the same word, "yashab," is used to refer to our dwelling in the shelter of God. As we continue to read through Psalm 91, we see some of God's examples of how He protects and cares for those who dwell in Him.

When we read these two verses in light of each other, we can almost picture dwelling closely with God during worship. We also learn from reading all of Psalm 91 that by loving God and calling on His name when we are trouble, He is our refuge and fortress.

Questions Sixteen and Seventeen

Because worship is our personal response to God, our reasons for worshiping will be different. Two commonalities we all share though is that God chooses to work through us and worship should lead to an expansion of God's Kingdom. To understand our part in the kingdom requires introspection and self-evaluation on our part. It's up to us to determine our spiritual gifts, our God-given talents, plus our passions and submit them to Jesus Christ. God is looking for submitted men and women to do mighty things. Worship is a great way to start.

■ Leader Notes

If you enjoyed this study, be sure to check out other studies in the Kingdom Living series at: ampelonpublishing.com